WHAT IS LOVE?

MIKE NOVOTNY

with bonus Bible study by Amber Albee Swenson

Published by Straight Talk Books
P.O. Box 301, Milwaukee, WI 53201
800.661.3311 • timeofgrace.org

Copyright © 2022 Time of Grace Ministry

All rights reserved. This publication may not be copied, photocopied, reproduced, translated, or converted to any electronic or machine-readable form in whole or in part, except for brief quotations, without prior written approval from Time of Grace Ministry.

Scripture is taken from THE HOLY BIBLE, NEW INTERNATIONAL VERSION®, NIV®. Copyright © 1973, 1978, 1984, 2011 by Biblica, Inc.® Used by permission. All rights reserved worldwide.

Printed in the United States of America
ISBN: 978-1-949488-55-5

TIME OF GRACE is a registered mark of Time of Grace Ministry.

Contents

Introduction 5

Show Tough or Tender Love? 7

Isn't Jesus on MY Side? 13

What's My First Love? 21

I'm Supposed to Love "Those" People? 27

The Descriptions of Love: A Bible Study 33

    Love Is Patient 35

    Love Is Kind 43

    Love Does Not Envy 52

    Love Does Not Boast, Is Not Proud 57

    Love Does Not Dishonor Others 64

    Love Is Not Self-Seeking 71

    Love Is Not Easily Angered 79

    Love Keeps No Record of Wrongs 87

    Love Does Not Delight in Evil 94

Introduction

Every good mother knows that love is a balance of tough and tender. In a healthy home, you'll hear a lot of, "Oh, come here, honey" and a lot of, "Because I said so." It has to be tough and tender. If a parent is too tough—rarely snuggling, hugging, complimenting, or expressing affection—that's not exactly love. But if a parent is too tender—babying, bulldozing on behalf of, and finding a Band-Aid for every boo-boo—that's not exactly love either. Because love is doing what's best. Sometimes what's best for a kid is tough—no screens; no dessert; "You get what you get, and you don't throw a fit." And sometimes what's best for a kid is tender—"It's been a hard day . . . who wants ice cream?" Tough and tender.

Every Christian knows that too. To love like Jesus, we must be both tough and tender. If a Christian is too tough—dropping truth bombs, commandment quoting, calling people to turn or burn—that's not exactly love. But if a Christian is too tender—"God loves you just as you are, so I'm never going to talk about your sin"—that's not love either. If love is doing what's best for our friends, our neighbors, our roommates, our families, then we have to figure out how to balance tough and tender.

Love is doing what's best.

That happened to me recently when I was walking downtown to a coffee shop. There, layered up in his old clothes, was a homeless man whom I knew. He asked, "Excuse me, Pastor, could I have a dollar?" What would you do? Be tough and tell him about the free resources and nonprofits that will help fix his real problems? Or be tender and take out your wallet?

Figuring out what is best, what is love, is kind of complicated. Like when you're frustrated with a member of your family—do you call a family meeting, even if it gets messy? Your roommate drinks not one but a few, not with friends but by himself, not on Fridays but on most days. What would love do? Your girlfriend is depressed and doesn't want to leave the house. Do you push her or put her desires first? Your daughter comes out as bisexual. Your city falls short of justice for all. Your church is stuck in its ways. What does love look like then? How tough? How tender? If God had a recipe, how many cups of tough and how many cups of tender would make love taste just right?

How much tough and how much tender? And to whom do I show love and how? Those are the questions I want to walk through with you in the chapters of this book. And after, you can work through the Bible study by Amber Albee Swenson to help you put what you've learned into practice.

Show Tough or Tender Love?

I want to start off by diving into one of the most famous sections of the whole Bible on love—1 Corinthians 13:4-8. Amber's Bible study on page 33 takes an even deeper dive into this section of Scripture, so please stick around for it! But for now, as we speed through its 16 descriptions of love (yes, 16!), I'm going to ask you if each one is tough or tender. Let's see how tough and how tender a Christian's love should be.

Here's where the apostle Paul starts his description: **"Love is patient."** Love takes a looooong time to get angry. Love slows down while your little brother ties his shoes, slows down to listen to an Alzheimer's patient tell the same story, smiles when the trainee in aisle 3 looks up the price of cilantro. Is that tough or tender? Tender.

Second, **"Love is kind."** It's nice, thoughtful, caring. Love gives a quiet compliment after a stressful season at work. Love shows up three months after the funeral just to check in. Tough or tender? Tender.

Third, **"It does not envy."** Love doesn't pout when other people get praised—when she starts as setter or he gets the promotion you wanted. "I don't want a monopoly on God's blessing. I'm happy for you because I want you to be blessed too." Tough or tender? Tender.

Fourth, **"It does not boast,"** and fifth, **"It is not proud."** No stat sharing, chest-thumping, or humble bragging. Love says, "I couldn't have gotten these grades without good teachers. I couldn't have gotten sober without my sponsor. I couldn't have done anything without you, without God." Tough or tender? Tender.

Sixth, **"It does not dishonor others."** Love doesn't want to embarrass others online or at the Monday meeting. "I honestly care about what other people think of you." That's love. Tough or tender? Tender.

Seventh, **"It is not self-seeking."** "I'd prefer, I'd choose, I want, but . . . you first. Honey, you feel loved by talking after work, by texting during the day? Not my jam, but you first. You feel loved by long hugs, back rubs, and making love? You first." Tough or tender? Tender.

Eighth, **"It is not easily angered."** Love rarely reaches for the caps lock. You don't have to walk on egg shells around love. Tough or tender? Tender.

Ninth, **"It keeps no record of wrongs."** Love is the opposite of cancel culture. It opens its arms for sinners who are sorry. It doesn't keep the stones of your sinful past within arm's reach to throw them back in your face. Love forgives. Tough or tender? Very tender.

Tenth, **"Love does not delight in evil."** Even when it happens to evil people. Love doesn't want unfair critics to be unfairly criticized because love loves justice for all, even them. Tough or tender? Tender.

Eleventh, love **"rejoices with the truth."** Love rejoices, smiles at, applauds, gets happy about the truth. Oh. Wait. Did you catch that word? *The.* Love doesn't rejoice with any and every kind of truth, with my truth and your truth. No, love only rejoices with *the* truth.

Love only rejoices with *the* truth.

And Jesus said, **"Father, your word is truth"** (John 17:17). Love won't applaud you if you're opposing the truth, because love can't lie. Is that tough or tender? Tough. So tough.

Twelfth, **"It always protects."** This phrase is tough to translate, but let's stick with "protect" for now. Protect implies something is in danger. You protect a quarterback from a blindside sack or protect your nephew from internet bullies. You have to stand up, fight, and defend to protect. Tough or tender? Tough.

Thirteenth and fourteenth, love **"always trusts"** and **"always hopes."** Love isn't overly skeptical or pessimistic. It trusts that God is going to win in the end. It has hope that Jesus will make all things right. Tough or tender? Tender.

Fifteenth and, finally, sixteenth, love **"always perseveres"** and **"love never fails."** The Greek word for "persevere" means to remain under pressure without giving up. Think of squatting at the gym or the final round of a workout class. You want to quit, but you don't. You keep loving, keep serving, even if you're sweating. You refuse to fail. Tough or tender? Tough.

Whew. You still with me? So is love tough or tender? Both. But how much of each? By my count—which is admittedly subjective—Paul lists 4 toughs and 12 tenders. One part tough to every three parts tender: 25% tough. Maybe we could write it like this—*Love is tough and TENDER.* It is both, but love is more one than the other.

Think of love like a juicy hamburger. Ever notice how meat has this breakdown of lean vs. fat? 30% fat or 20% or 10%. Why is that? Because fat is our friend . . . but not our best friend. Fat adds flavor and moisture, but too much fat and that burger is nasty. You need both but way more of one than the other. That's what makes a burger good. And that's what makes love good too. Does love need to be tough? For sure. But just a little tough. According to Paul, love is mostly tender.

So what does this mean for you and me? First, tough does not equate with hate. When someone gives you tough love, don't quote Taylor Swift and think about how haters will hate and you can shake them off. Because that's not hate. When someone so loves the truth that they can't support your truth . . . when they share the tough news that God doesn't agree with your truth, that's not hate. When a friend wants to talk about your attitude about school or your drinking or your Snaps . . . when your mom reaches for her Bible and wants to talk about church, about staying connected . . . when your brother or sister doesn't immediately take your side when you want to file for divorce, don't huff and don't puff. I know it's tough, but love is tough. I dare you to ask someone this week, "Do you feel you can talk to me about tough things?" If so, then your life will be filled with love.

Second, tend toward tender. Think about your classmates, your coworkers, your significant other, your friends, and even your enemies, and tend toward tender. They're all sinners. They all sin daily. Which means you logically could call them out every day and give them tough love. But love is a little tough and lots of tender. Look for ways to be tender this week, to be patient with his personality, to be kind toward her quirks, to trust that they didn't have evil intentions. Save 1 Corinthians 13:4-8 on your phone or write it on a note card and ask God, "Help me love like you. I won't be perfect, but help me try to give them a glimpse of your love."

Tend toward tender.

Back in the 1970s, two doctors wanted to see if they could predict which married couples would stay married. They set up an experiment in which a couple would talk about a relationship problem for 15 minutes. Then, after watching the tapes, the doctors would predict who would stay together and who would eventually get divorced. They followed up with the couples nine years later and learned that their predictions turned out to be right more than 90% of the time!

How did they make their guesses? They looked for the ratio between positive and negative interactions. How often did couples laugh/agree/listen/empathize/express gratitude and how often did they criticize, cross their arms, interrupt, etc.? What they found was that couples that stayed married had five positive moments for every one negative moment. In other words, happy, loving couples were both tough and tender, but way more tender.

Finally (this is my favorite part): *God is tough and TENDER.* Look at this amazing verse: **"God is love"** (1 John 4:8). This is what God is like. Is our Father tough with us? At times. He calls us out, tells us to repent, and refuses to let his kids run the kingdom.

But for every time he is tough, he is so tender with us. God is patient when we struggle day after day with the same sin. God is kind enough to give us the sun and to give us his Son. Jesus isn't boastful but humble, so humble that he would die so that we could be loved every instant by God himself. Instead of being easily angered with us, Jesus climbed up on a cross for us so that God would never keep a record of our wrongs (can you imagine that?!). Never! No record! Anything that would have made God mad is gone, nailed to that tree. God doesn't delight in evil; he delivered us from it. God rejoices with the truth. The truth that you are forgiven. That you are clean. That you don't have to pay him back. That, through faith in Jesus, you are his child. That makes him happy. That's why his face shines on us when he blesses and keeps us. Jesus always protect us. You might be afraid of death or feel ashamed of your past, but Jesus protects you from all that. You're going to be okay because you can always trust Jesus; you can always hope in Jesus because Jesus always perseveres and never fails.

Our God is love—tough, yes, and so, so tender.

Just ask Moses. About 3,500 years ago, the prophet Moses stood with the people of Israel at Mt. Sinai and heard, for the first time ever, God's Ten Commandments. The Israelites were scared because of the fire and the clouds and the tough love of a God who would command them and judge them. But right after God gave them the First Commandment—You shall have no other gods—he said something that should have grabbed their attention. God gave his people a number, a ratio, a hint of his loving heart. God said this: **"I, the Lord your God, am a jealous God, punishing the children for the sin of the parents to the third and fourth generation of those who hate me . . ."** (Exodus 20:5). God is tough. He is jealous, fiercely protective of his people; God does punish. When we hate God enough to repeat the sins of our parents without saying sorry, he will punish us. For three or four generations. But do you know what he said next? He said, **". . . but showing love to a thousand generations of those who love me and keep my commandments"** (verse 6). A thousand?! He punishes three or four but shows love to a thousand! That's crazy!

But that sounds about right. Because love is tough, but, more than anything, love is tender. Just like God. Because God is love.

Isn't Jesus on MY Side?

In late 2020, Netflix released a musical movie called *The Prom*. Have you seen it? It's about a lesbian teenager who plans to bring her girlfriend to the prom until the religious folks shut it down. The cross-necklaced principal and the churchgoing students won't stand for such sin . . . which is where the Broadway actors come in. Fresh from New York, they try to change some hearts in this small Indiana town. The turning point happens in the local mall where a song and dance number breaks out (obviously; it's a musical) and one of the Broadway guys belts about . . . Jesus. And love. And it's really catchy. And it works.

In American culture, it is rare to hear people say, "Jesus was wrong. Here's what's right." No, what is much more common is to claim that Jesus is on this side, on our side, on the side of love. Have you noticed this?

The traditional crowd says that Jesus loved traditional marriage; male and female; sex as a sacred, post-vow gift from God. The progressive crowd says that, no, Jesus loved breaking the status quo and judged people who judged other people. The church people say that Jesus loved the church, the organization of religion. The not-into-church people say that, no, Jesus went off on those who went through the motions and believed that being in a building somehow blessed you. Some say Jesus was tough on sinners, calling people to repentance and threatening them with the fires of hell. Others say Christ was tender, that you'd most often find the Messiah on the margins, blessing the broken, defending the oppressed, including the excluded.

So what's the truth about Jesus? If Jesus is God and God

is love, then Jesus is the best example of love ever. So where is the One who is Love? Where would Jesus stand on today's toughest questions? That's the question I want to try to answer in this chapter.

Thankfully, John can help. John was one of Jesus' best friends who not only wrote a biography about Jesus but focused that biography on the topic of love. Love one another? That's in John. God so loved the world? That's in John too. Matthew, Mark, and Luke combined use the word *love* 36 times. John uses it 39 times by himself! So I want to go through the book of John at warp speed and figure out how Jesus, the God of love, actually lived. Is your brain ready? I hope so, because here's what we find in the 21 chapters of John:

Jesus is the best example of love ever.

In John chapter 1, Jesus is described as **"full of grace and truth"** (verse 14). He never watered down the truth, not once, and yet he was filled to the brim with undeserved love. That's why, when he met Nathanael, a skeptic who mocked Jesus' small-town roots, he loved him and invited him to follow him.

In John chapter 2, Jesus went to a wedding. When the wine ran out, he had compassion on the hosts and did his first miracle, turning water into a rich red wine like the guests had never tasted. Then Jesus went to Jerusalem and threw a temple tantrum, flipping over tables and cracking a whip, disgusted at the corruption of the church.

In John chapter 3, Jesus called out a Pharisee named Nicodemus: **"You are Israel's teacher and do you not understand these things?"** (verse 10)—and then, in the same conversation, tenderly said, **"God so loved the world that he gave his one and only Son"** (verse 16).

In John chapter 4, Jesus met the outcast of outcasts, a

mixed-race woman with multiple divorces who was holding on to heresies and living with her latest guy. And he was so tough with her. **"Go, call your husband,"** he commanded (verse 16), knowing she didn't have one. And then he was so tender with her, offering her "water" that could satisfy her soul, which was so good she raced into town to tell everyone about Jesus.

In John chapter 5, Jesus met a man who had been disabled for 38 years, and he healed him! Can you imagine? Then, five verses later, Jesus said, **"Stop sinning or something worse may happen to you"** (verse 14). Can you imagine?

In John chapter 6, Jesus had compassion on five thousand hungry men. Then, after the Tupperware was filled with leftovers, Jesus preached a sermon so savage that all of them—all of them!—left.

In John chapter 7, Jesus accused the church people, **"Not one of you keeps God's law"** (verse 19). Then he shouted to the crowds, "If you are thirsty—thirsty for life, for love, for God—come to me" (verse 37).

In John chapter 8, church leaders dragged a woman caught in adultery before Jesus. **"Let any one of you who is without sin be the first to throw a stone at her,"** Jesus dared them (verse 7). When they left, he smiled, **"Neither do I condemn you."** But before she left, he added, **"Go now and leave your life of sin"** (verse 11).

In John chapter 9, Jesus made a blind man see and then said, "If you all don't think you are sinners who need to be saved, you are blind, and I have come to judge you."

In John chapter 10, Jesus claimed to be the Good Shepherd, the one who would lay down his life to give us life to the full. Then he preached so hard that many said he was raving mad and demon possessed!

In John chapter 11, Jesus attended his friend's funeral. In

one of his tenderest moments, Jesus wept. And then he got angry. Furious at the existence of death and the unbelief of the crowd, he stomped over to the tomb and demanded that his dead friend live again.

In John chapter 12, Jesus was tender with Mary, allowing her to anoint his body with perfume. Then he was tough with Judas, who whined about her waste of money.

In John chapter 13, Jesus washed his disciples' feet, even Judas, the "friend" who would stab him in the back. After he dried his hands, Jesus spoke of betrayal and denial, and the guys with the clean feet were stunned and sad.

In John chapter 14, Jesus revealed that his Father's house had many rooms and that he was going to prepare a place for us. Then he taught that people who don't care about his commandments, don't love him and have no place with him.

In John chapter 15, Jesus spoke about love. Lots of it. "I have loved you," he said. "I chose you," he smiled. "I have called you friends," he said. But he also said, **"If you do not remain in me, you are like a branch that is thrown away and withers; such branches are picked up, thrown into the fire and burned"** (verse 6).

In John chapter 16, Jesus predicted, "You will leave me all alone." A verse later—one verse!—he said, **"But take heart! I have overcome the world"** (verse 33).

In John chapter 17, Jesus tenderly prayed for his friends because they would still be in this world, a world that would hate them.

In John chapter 18, Jesus lovingly held back his divine power so the guards could arrest him; but while under arrest, he rebuked Peter for his sword swinging, the Pharisees for their false charges, and Pontius Pilate for betraying the truth.

In John chapter 19, Jesus tenderly told John to take care of mother, Mary. Then he died.

In John chapter 20, Jesus rose from the dead and, in one of the tenderest moments in history, said to his grieving friend, **"Mary"** (verse 16). Days later, he scolded Thomas, **"Stop doubting and believe"** (verse 27). And then, finally, in John chapter 21, Jesus made breakfast for the apostles and put Peter on the spot: "Do you love me? Do you? Do you?" Yet he still invited Peter, despite his triple denial, to take care of God's precious people.

The end. Whew! You still with me? That's what John, the one whom Jesus loved, wrote about Jesus, the God of love. So what did we learn? We learned that Jesus was tough. Savage. Brutal. With whom? With all of them. With the church men, the Samaritan woman, with the disabled guy, the grieving girls, the adulteress, the religious, with Judas and Peter and Pilate and Thomas, with the greedy, the sexually immoral, the doubters, and the cowards. Jesus was tough with them all. AND! Jesus was tender. So tender. **Jesus is tough and tender.** Unbelievably tender to an embarrassed couple at their wedding, to a broken woman who thought she didn't belong, to a disabled man who had given up hope, to his mother, to his denier. Jesus was tender with them all. So what is Jesus like? Highlight this: *Jesus is tough and tender.* Not with some. With all. With us. With you.

Kind of like Ken. A few years ago, I was invited to talk at a special event hosted at a Milwaukee high school. Think suit and tie, catered food, kind of fancy. Before the guests arrived, however, I looked down and noticed an inch of my thigh. That's right; my suit pants had pulled apart at the seam the day of the event, revealing what no one in the room wanted to see. And I didn't have backup pants. What was I supposed to do?! Stand behind the podium all night? Try to cover up the tear with my hand? Not the best impression for the new lead speaker of Time of Grace! But then Ken walked into the room. He was the president of the high school, a man equally intelligent and assertive, not the quiet type you forget is in the room. But that day, when he saw my situation, Ken said to me, "Come here." I went back to his office—and this is going to sound awkward, but it wasn't—I went into the bathroom and handed the pants out the crack in the door and then—get this—the president himself got out a sewing kit, sat down, and stitched up my pants. I'm not making this up! The one in authority, the guy who makes the tough decisions, was tender enough to save me.

Just like Jesus. Jesus is tough, and Jesus is tender, and both parts will surprise you. Let's apply those two things before I finish up this chapter. Jesus is tough. The most loving biography in the Bible proves it. If the real Jesus was in that Netflix movie, he would say to the church kids, "You hypocrites. You're sleeping around, watching porn, and judging her for being gay? You need to look in the mirror, judge yourself, and worry about you." And then Jesus would turn to the girl and say, "I love you. I want you in heaven. But if anyone wants to be my disciple, they must deny themselves, take up their cross, and follow me. Will you?"

The Sunday after the prom, Jesus would stop by the church and warn the pastor about people-pleasing, about enjoying the perks of pastoral ministry without doing the hard work of being a good shepherd, of searching for the lost, of going to war against the wolves, about carrying lambs with compassion. After church, Jesus might head out to brunch and ask why people who claim to be close to God aren't close to God's Word, God's people, or gathering around God's truth. He would ask who deceived them into thinking that a churchless faith is even an option to God. And, perhaps, on the way there, Jesus would buy a homeless man a sandwich and warn him that unrepentant drunks cannot be saved. If you've ever wondered why Jesus only had 120 followers after dozens of miracles, a perfect life, a sacrificial death, and a glorious resurrection, this is why—Jesus was tough. He still is.

And Jesus is so tender. If you were raised with religion but missed being reborn, like Nicodemus, Jesus is tender with you. God loves you so much. If you only knew! If you have been divorced, are sleeping with someone who isn't your spouse, like the Samaritan woman, Jesus is tender with you. There is living water for you. If you are on disability, hungry, poor, or just got caught in an affair, Jesus is tender enough to see you, to feed you, to invite you, to not condemn you. If you have been blind to God's love for you, Jesus wants to make you see it. If you have felt invisible, Jesus wants to call you by name. If you are dying, Jesus wants to be your life. He will wash your feet, wash away your sins, and make you clean. He will prepare a place for you, call you his friend, give you his Spirit, and pray that God would protect you. Because he suffered for you, he died for you, he finished it for you, and he rose for you. He is appearing to you today, like Mary and Thomas and Peter, inviting you to believe in him, giving you a purpose, saying to you, like he did on that glorious Sunday: "Mary. Mike. Maya. Marcus." He knows your name. He does. He's Jesus. He is love.

I think that's why people love the book *Gentle and Lowly* by Dane Ortlund. A quarter million copies were sold in a single year, which is insane for a Christian book. The author focused his entire message on a single passage, on the only time in the entire gospels when Jesus tells us what his own heart is like. Here's what Jesus said: **"Come to me, all you who are weary and burdened, and I will give you rest. Take my yoke upon you and learn from me, for I am gentle and humble in heart,**

and you will find rest for your souls" (Matthew 11:28,29).

Is Jesus tough? For sure. Is he tender? gentle? lowly? Thank God, yes. Jesus is tough and tender because Jesus is love. John knew that. And now you do too.

What's My First Love?

Under the cover of darkness, the tall silhouettes crept across the perfect yard of a suburban home and toward the front door. Glancing at the others, one of the men removed a small bottle from his pocket. They held their breath as he uncapped the bottle and poured the pungent liquid all over the doorknob and the welcome mat below it. Before they needed to breathe, the men took off, whispering to their toilet paper-throwing friends that the job was done and, as quietly as they had arrived, they escaped into the night.

True story. I know because I was there. That was me. But the other guy started it.

When I was a teenager, my friends and I got into roller hockey, which is why we were ecstatic when the city paved some smooth blacktop right in our neighborhood. But the neighbor who lived on our street wasn't. Neighbor guy loved his yard—his lush, level grass—which is why things got ugly. We rolled up (literally), set up goals, and played hockey for hours. When the ball jumped the curb every few minutes, we trudged on top of his grass to get it, clunky skates pressing into the soil, which is when he would come out his front door to yell at us to get off his yard. That's why the next school homecoming we decided to leave him a gift—all organic! (I'm sensing you're not taking my side on this one, and I'm thankful that Jesus saves teenage sinners!)

I'm telling you this because that conflict was deeply spiritual. That's what St. Augustine would say. Augustine, a Christian from the fourth century, suggested that most of your life, your spiritual life and your emotional life, can be explained by putting the things you love in order. What you love most, what you love second most, etc. In this case, my friends and I loved our game more than we loved that guy's yard. But that guy loved his yard more than he loved our game. We had different orders, different priorities, which led to frustration, anger, and a lack of love.

Have you ever thought about the order of your loves? Maybe thinking about Legos will help. Imagine a stack of six building blocks, each labeled with one of the following: family, friends, health, work, school, and God. These are all good things, right? But the question—the deeply spiritual question, the question that determines so much about you—is this: What do you love the most? In what order do you stack them? When you have to choose between family and friends, which is your first love? For example, if your family wants to talk to you during dinner but your friends are blowing up your phone, which will you choose? Or if you could make six figures doing this work but you wouldn't have much time for friends, would you take the job? If you could either spend the summer with family up north or worship with your church family in town, which would you choose? If you got super serious about your health but your grades at school slipped, what then? If you had to choose an order to stack your Legos, what would your order be? And what would theirs be? What matters most to your mom, your brother, your significant other? How does their order compare to yours? And how does that affect the way you love each other . . . or don't?

God talks about the order of our loves and what that means for our lives. We're going to look to Moses, then the psalmists, and then to Jesus to get our loves in the right order.

Moses was the guy who first got the Ten Commandments about 3,500 years ago. Have you heard of the Ten Commandments? Remember the First Commandment? If you don't, that's okay. Here's what God actually said in

Exodus 20:3: **"You shall have no other gods before me."** Before me. There is only one true God, but when God gave the First Commandment, he included an order. He wanted to be on the top of the Lego stack. Nothing was before him.

The reformer Martin Luther lived about five hundred years ago, and he didn't want Christians to rattle off the right answers without really thinking, so he wrote a catechism, a book filled with the question: What does this mean? On page 1, Luther started with the First Commandment and then asked, "What does this mean?" His answer: *"We should fear, love, and trust in God above all things."* Above all things. #1. Our first love. You might fear losing your health or your money or your friends or your family, but fear God even more. You might love your career, your mom, your son, but love God even more. You might trust in your savings, your friendships, your family to give you a good life, but trust in God even more. Luther picked up on Moses, who wanted you to make God your first love.

Love God even more.

But why? Why would you make God the most important thing in your life? The psalmists knew. The book of Psalms is the most loving book in the entire Bible. The word *love* shows up 161 times; that's quadruple the amount of *love* that you'd find in the gospel of John. And notice what kind of love the psalms say makes God worthy of being your #1: **"Within your temple, O God, we meditate on your unfailing love"** (48:9). **"But I trust in your unfailing love"** (13:5). **"Satisfy us in the morning with your unfailing love"** (90:14). **"How priceless is your unfailing love, O God!"** (36:7). Why put God on top? Because God is the only one who never fails. Do people fail you at work? Do friends let you down? Do your knees ache and your mind get anxious? Yes, everything fails except God's love. That's why God is worthy of being at the top, your first love.

Jesus knew that too. When his friends were worried about health and money and family, he said, **"Do not worry. . . . But seek first his kingdom and his righteousness, and all these things will be given to you as well"** (Matthew 6:25,33). Seek *first* the kingdom of God. Get your heart to that place where you think about God and how he offers safety from all your spiritual enemies. How he forgives you for that (yes, that). How he has a place in heaven for everyone who believes in Jesus. How he loves you so much he refuses to keep a record of your wrongs. Seek that first, and you'll have something better than six figures or a six-pack. You'll have the peace that other people don't have and don't even understand.

God is our first love.

So what do we learn from Moses and the psalmists and Jesus? Let's summarize it this way: God is our first love. He deserves to come first because he is God, and God is the source of unfailing love.

That's what inspired Lauren Daigle to write one of her hit songs. She was about to record all the songs for her debut album, which would later become platinum with one million sales, but something didn't feel quite right. She felt like the record was missing something. She was restless and anxious, so she decided to take a nap since she couldn't focus on her work. When she woke up, someone had messaged her on Instagram and included the words of Matthew 6:33: **"But seek first his kingdom."** The next day she met with her team, told them about the passage, and they wrote a new song that would be the first song on her album. They decided to call it "First." It's about wanting to seek God first more than anything.

So where do you go from here? What do you do with this? Here are three quick applications. First, figure out your order. Think about your life, your schedule, your budget. When you have to pick, what comes first? When you can't do both, which do you do? This might convict you—"Oh. I've been putting work over my own family and friendships." Or this might comfort you—"It's okay that I'm not the best in my class because I'm sleeping instead of studying until 1:00 a.m." You're not God. You can't be good at everything. So be good at the somethings that matter most.

Like seeking God. I really love it when I see people in church on Sunday because it's the first day of the week. And I know the first thing some people do each day is pray. I know that when some get paid, the first thing they do is give. And I know some, before the gym, before work, before school, open the Bible and seek God. I love that. I love seeing my members in church. I love knowing that people are watching at home, joining me online. Because when you go to church or open your Bible in the morning, you get God, and when you get God, you get unfailing love. This week, a thousand things will fail. Something will go wrong. Someone will go wrong. How good is it—how priceless, how satisfying—when you start your week and your day with something that doesn't fail, that can't

What small step could you take?

fail? If you've never done that, never sought God first, what small step could you take today? According to Jesus, you won't regret it.

Second, figure out their order. Think about what the people in your life prioritize in their lives. Because understanding what people love helps us decrease the hate. My roller hockey neighbor didn't hate kids; he just loved his yard. I wish I would have known that. We need to know this, or hate will tear us apart. When someone supports local law enforcement, they don't hate minorities. They really don't.

And when someone kneels during the national anthem, they don't hate veterans. They really don't. In those moments, they are just prioritizing differently. If we forget that, if others don't share our order, hate can happen so quickly. We can't let that happen. Not as Christians. Not as people who will be known by their love. I'll have more on this idea in the next chapter. You'll have to keep reading!

Finally, thank God for his order. Two thousand years ago, God came into our world in flesh and blood, and his name was Jesus. Since he was God, Jesus had the right to be first. But he didn't prioritize his rights. Because more than he loved comfort, he loved you. More than he loved a pain-free life, he loved you. More than he loved his own life, he loved you. He put you first. *God* put *you* first! Imagine that.

Recently, I attended a big Christian conference in Indianapolis and managed to get a front-row seat to hear a breakout session by Nancy Guthrie. If you don't know that name, Nancy is a prolific Christian author with over two dozen books under her belt, which is why they put her breakout session in a big ballroom. That's why I was surprised to look up before the session started and see . . . Nancy Guthrie. There she was, walking through the room, introducing herself to total strangers, asking their names, giving them COVID-approved elbow bumps, and thanking them for coming. "What is she doing down here?" I wondered. The one who deserved to be up on stage was right there among us. It was beautiful because it was like Jesus, the Savior who didn't prioritize his rights but instead your relationship with God.

Why do we love God first? Because he started it! We love him first because he first loved us.

I'm Supposed to Love "Those" People?

Brain scientist David Eagleman once conducted an experiment on empathy. His team scanned the brain activity of a person who was watching videos of another person getting poked in the hand by a needle. Each time the needle poked, they could read what was happening in the brain of the observer. But then, a twist. They labeled each hand to be poked with a religion—this is the hand of a Christian; this is the hand of a Muslim; this is an atheist; this is a Hindu. Guess what happened? When the needle poked one of "their people," the observer's brain burst with activity. But when it poked one of "those people," nothing. "Your brain just doesn't care about 'them,'" Dr. Eagleman concluded.

This whole book has been about love, but there's one big thing we still need to cover—*them*. Those people. The people who don't believe what you believe or behave like you behave. The folks on the other side of the aisle; the other side of the debate; the ones who don't share your values, your priorities, your faith. You know all about "your people," so let's talk about "those people."

If I gave you a second, could you figure out who those people are, the ones who instantly increase your stress level? Those people could be an entire demographic—conservatives, liberals, Muslims, evangelicals, straight/white/cisgender men, loud-and-proud/love-is-love/married lesbian women, Black Lives Matter protestors, or Planned Parenthood protestors—or they could be individuals. That one girl from your class. That one guy from your job. Your ex. Your in-laws. The grouchy neighbor with the perfect yard. Thinking of someone right now?

One of the hardest things about love is logic. Here's what I mean: The Bible says that love is tough and love is tender. The Bible also says that everyone is a sinner. Which means that you can, logically, be tough with them. You can call them out and be correct. What happens, however, is that love starts to pick and choose: tough with some, tender with others, critical of those people, compassionate with my people. And the result is that everyone is loving . . . kind of. Loving toward our people. Tender with our people. But not with those people. And, it turns out, they act a lot like us: tender with their own and tough with us.

Jesus knew all about this. In groups and out groups, our people and those people, this was the status quo in his day . . . until Jesus blew that all up. What Jesus taught—most important, what Jesus did—is a game changer for love, for life, for us. That's what I want us to look at in Matthew chapter 5.

Let's start in verse 43: **"You have heard that it was said, 'Love your neighbor and hate your enemy.'"** That's what people said in the first century. You love your neighbors, and you hate your enemies; you love your fellow Jews, and you hate the Romans, the pagans, the back-stabbing tax collectors. Amen to that, Jesus.

"But I tell you, love your enemies and pray for those who persecute you" (verse 44). Wait, what? Love? Pray for the people with different priorities and those who persecute me? The ones who come after me and make my life harder? Jesus, I don't like the guy who forwards me too many emails, and you want me to love my enemies? Why would I do that?

Here's why: **"That you may be children of your Father in heaven. He causes his sun to rise on the evil and the good, and sends rain on the righteous and the unrighteous"** (verse 45). Why love them? Because God does. Because God loves the evil and the good. Because God blesses the godly and the godless. And when you stop picking and choosing and start unconditionally loving, you will look a lot like your Father in heaven.

If you look at the weather app on your phone right now, it'll give you a particular temperature. Now what if your teenage son, the atheist whom you work with, your best friend's grandma, your gay neighbor, the local librarian, and the imam from the mosque next to your gym look at the same app right now? Will the temperature be the same? Yes! Why? Because God sends the sun and the rain on the good and the bad, the young and the old, on your people and those people. Meaning—God loves the world.

If you struggle with loving someone, maybe you should check the weather more often. Watch the rain green up the grass of the guy you don't like. See the tan on that girl from school because the Father brought the sun up for her too. Let creation preach the unconditional love of God into your heart: The sun shines on sinners. The rain falls on the fallen. **God loves his friends and his enemies.** The sky is blue for the boastful. The grass is green for the greedy. Because God loves his friends and his enemies. He loves the world.

Imitating that is way better than this: **"If you love those who love you, what reward will you get? Are not even the tax collectors doing that? And if you greet only your own people, what are you doing more than others? Do not even pagans do that?"** (verses 46,47). That's tough love from Jesus. The people you don't like are a lot like you. They love their friends. They greet their people. You don't have to be a Christian to love like that; that's common. That is unremarkably average.

No, here's a higher calling: **"Be perfect, therefore, as your heavenly Father is perfect"** (verse 48). Imitate the perfect love of your heavenly Father who doesn't pick and choose but instead loves the entire world. He loves them. He loves you.

My wife, Kim, and I had the chance to put this passage into practice last weekend. I talked at a wedding that was, by far, the most diverse gathering of people I've ever spoken to. Sitting on one side were the very conservative, very religious people, many of whom worked full time for Christian ministries. Sitting on the other side were the not conservative, not religious people. The friendly bare-chested guy in full makeup, leopard-printed velour suit, and high heels. The girl who didn't realize I was the pastor until after she had used Jesus' name and the f-word in the same sentence. What an amazing chance to be like our Father, to not huddle in "our" corner, to introduce ourselves to one another, to listen, to love, to pursue the perfect love of a Father who doesn't pick and choose. I'm going to write it this way: Love one an"other." A reminder that God calls us to love the "other."

Isn't that what made Jesus so amazing? Two thousand years ago, the world was a dark place. Everyone picked their side—Jews vs. Gentiles, Pharisees vs. Sadducees, rich vs. poor—and everyone loved their people. But then came the light of Jesus, "God with us," walking among us. He was Love living on earth. And this Jesus was so different, crossing borders, social norms, expectations, being tough and tender with all, loving the world. He called men and women to follow him, healed the diseases of Jews and Gentiles, forgave Pharisees and Samaritans, and then he died. Not for some but for all. For God so loved the world that he gave his one and only Son, the Lamb of God who takes away not only our sins but the sins of the whole world. If you are a Christian, it's only because God loved "those people." Before you and I were his children, before we believed, while we were still sinners, he loved us. He sought us and saved us. When God wasn't your first love, he loved you first. My story and your story, the story of every Christian is of a gracious God who refused to pick and choose but instead gave up everything to love everyone.

This is our calling. It will not be natural. There may not be any earthly reward. But we can be little lights in a very dark place, people who don't pick, people who just love. We can be people who are tough, yes, but who tend toward tender, not just with our people but with those people. Jesus said love them, lend money to them, give to them, be good to them. If you're not sure where to start, how about with a prayer? "Father, help me love them like you first loved me."

How beautiful would that be? I think I know because I've seen it up close. Back in the summer of 2020, I got a glimpse of this kind of love. It was the height of the racial protests in my city, and over a thousand people had packed into our downtown square, seeking justice for all. So I went first with my daughters and then a few hours later on my own. I made my way up next to the stage where I could see behind the scenes, listen to the organizers, and scan the crowd where fully uniformed police officers stood on the edges and, I imagine, on edge. But then one of the leaders of the protest, a young Black man, got on the mic as the DJ started the music, and he said, "I don't care about the color of your skin; we are about to dance. So I need a police officer to come up here and dance with us." My neck snapped over to the two barrel-chested, Caucasian officers to my left, watching as they whispered to each other, guns on their hips. And then I was shocked when they both smiled and started walking toward the stage. The "Cha Cha Slide" started and—forgive me for the stereotype but—Black people can dance. And these cops . . . couldn't. But they did. In a sea of black and brown skin, two white men tried their best to dance. Because love is kind. Love is not self-seeking. Love is not self-selecting. That's why love never fails.

God's love doesn't pick and choose.

I glanced down at my feet after the dance was done and noticed a sign left by a supporter. It was just a Bible quote from Psalm 103—**"The Lord works righteousness and justice for all the oppressed"** (verse 6). For all. That sounds right. Because God's love doesn't pick and choose. It is tough and tender with us all.

As members of the family of God, may you and I love like that, just as our Father first loved us.

The Descriptions of Love: A Bible Study

First Corinthians chapter 13 is famous for its words on love. Verses 4–8 are almost poetic in their definition of love. In the first chapter of this book, I walked you through the 16 descriptions of love found in these verses. Now in the following Bible study, my friend and colleague Amber Albee Swenson looks more closely at those descriptions and what they mean for you and how you love others. As you head into the second part of this book, keep pondering what you learned in the first four chapters and how you can apply it to your everyday life.

—Pastor Mike

Love is patient, love is kind. It does not envy, it does not boast, it is not proud. It does not dishonor others, it is not self-seeking, it is not easily angered, it keeps no record of wrongs. Love does not delight in evil but rejoices with the truth. It always protects, always trusts, always hopes, always perseveres. Love never fails.

1 Corinthians 13:4-8

Love Is Patient

A fairly decent gauge of patience is a person's response to children and the elderly. If you live long enough, chances are you won't be able to keep up. In old age, dwindling hearing makes it hard to catch the whole conversation. Strength fades, and so does physical and mental speed. Family members who gently and lovingly help their parents into a wheelchair or up the stairs, who slow down and lean in, have learned to love the elderly well.

Patience is not a strength of mine. Too many mornings were rushed in our home as everyone scurried to the bus. Too many Sundays started with frenzied commands. Far worse was the exasperation I expressed all too often when my children didn't understand my commands or weren't going as fast as I wanted them to go.

God put 1 Corinthians 13:4 in the Bible for me and anyone who shares my disposition. I would have been like the disciples, rebuking the parents who brought their children to Jesus. "Jesus has more important things to do. Why are you wasting his time? Don't you know who this is?"

Jesus didn't see blessing children as a waste of time. In fact, he became indignant and said, "**'Let the little children come to me, and do not hinder them, for the kingdom of God belongs to such as these. Truly I tell you, anyone who will not receive the kingdom of God like a little child will never enter it.' And he took the children in his arms, placed his hands on them and blessed them**" (Mark 10:14-16).

Jesus was patient with the mothers and the children because people matter to God. Being patient with the people in our lives—whether they're our children or parents or neighbors or the driver in front of us—isn't a waste of our time either. When we're patient, we show them they matter not only to us but to God.

Sin is at the root of impatience. My sinful nature thinks my time is more important than someone else's. My goals, my expectations, my time frame is all that should be considered. And here's the darkest truth of my impatience. Sometimes I rush everyone else so I can finish what I want and/or think I need to finish in order to indulge in my selfish behaviors. I'm impatient to get home from work so I can get my comfy pants on and scroll through my phone. I don't have time to deal with someone's problems, but I can fit in an episode or two of my favorite show.

With which of your acquaintances do you tend to become impatient?

Which circumstances often lead to you losing your patience?

It's one thing to get impatient when someone is taking their time or is slow. It's another thing altogether to learn to be patient with people spiritually. It would be nice if when a person was heading in the wrong direction, all it took was a quick conversation and they admitted the error of their way and repented. All too often we have to learn to wait, like the father waiting and watching for his prodigal son.

I don't know why change so often takes time. It's easy, in the waiting, to give up and assume repentance will never happen. Far better to watch and pray and **"be patient, bearing with one another in love"** (Ephesians 4:2).

When our loved ones wander away from God, they are in the middle of a spiritual battle. Maybe they've grown up knowing the Lord, but God's way seemed dull. Or maybe they got tired of always being the odd man out, and they just wanted to be like everyone else. Or maybe they dove headfirst into any number of sins because they succumbed to the temptation of worldly pleasures and found it to be pleasurable. Or maybe they are just frail, and addiction is the zone they go to for comfort.

It's easy to see the inconvenience and hurt and the many times you've hoped only to be disappointed as reason to wash your hands of the person forever. If we're not careful, the other person becomes the enemy.

Satan is the real enemy. He's the one behind the tempting. Satan and his army of angels work hard to keep your loved one seduced and blinded. As soon as we understand this, we can battle *for* our loved one, not against them.

The Word will refuel us.

Since the battle takes place in the spiritual realm, we'll need spiritual weapons to battle with. Prayer will be our lifeline, asking God for what we need every day. The Holy Spirit will build us up and strengthen us to persevere. The Word will refuel us when we're ready to give up and lose hope and we don't know how to go on.

Through prayer we'll ask God to use all his resources to open our loved one's eyes. And the Holy Spirit will need to rekindle their faith. Love will propel us to treat the person as someone loved by God who is weak and frail and needs our help.

The book of Jude says, **"Be merciful to those who doubt; save others by snatching them from the fire; to others show mercy, mixed with fear—hating even the clothing stained by corrupted flesh"** (22-23).

Instead of losing our patience with the spiritually weak or lost, we need to remember the eternal consequence and pray, while pressing on with mercy, love, and grace. That's the way Jesus did it. Remember when Pastor Mike walked quickly through the chapters of the book of John (see pages 14-17)? Jesus was patient with Nicodemus when he didn't understand. Jesus met him in the night to explain what confused him. Jesus was patient with the woman at the well, and in his weariness, he made time for her. He took time out of his day to go back to the man he had healed and warned him to quit sinning. These things were done out of patience, not disgust, and out of love, not judgment. And that is just the first five chapters of the book of John!

And, of course, we'll be driven to patience as we realize how many times God and his children have been patient with us. Too many times I took longer than I should have to turn from sin, but God continued to work as my parents and others prayed.

We all have friends and loved ones who are not in a good spiritual place. Write their names and situations below.

How long has it been since you reached out? How can you make time in the next few days?

It's good for us to remember also that God patiently waits for us to do the kingdom work he has for us to do. First Peter 3:20 reminds us that **"God waited patiently in the days of Noah while the ark was being built."** We aren't certain how long exactly it took for Noah to build the ark (other than it was less than 120 years), but God waited patiently while he did so. The earth was a mess. God pronounced judgment, and he waited.

We don't know the particulars of Noah's life, but we know

he wasn't consumed with the latest Netflix series or changing his Snapchat avatar. No doubt his life had its own distractions. He had a wife and three married children. The daughters-in-law's families weren't saved. How much time was spent getting to know them and trying to make them understand there was room on the ark?

Are you clear about what God has for you to do?

Every day we get to decide how to spend the 16 or so waking hours we have. God gave Noah the task of building an ark. Are you clear about what God has for you to do?

If you're married, taking care of your spouse is part of your kingdom work. If you have children, it will take time to train them to know and love the Lord. If you have parents and neighbors and friends, God calls you to care for and encourage them.

Ephesians 2:10 reminds us that God also created us with specific traits and abilities to do specific tasks. **"For we are God's handiwork, created in Christ Jesus to do good works, which God prepared in advance for us to do."**

It's baffling to think that God chose for us to be born at this point and place in time because he had specific kingdom work for us to do. Are you doing it, or would it be said of you, "and God waited patiently"?

Maybe it's time to reprioritize. Maybe you have some unbelieving friends or relatives you need to make a priority. Maybe you have been putting off a specific assignment from God. Maybe you've lost your zeal entirely.

Every time I get sick I'm reminded what a blessing health is. When I'm incapacitated in bed or on the couch, I can't wait to be up doing things. I reevaluate how I'm spending my time. As soon as I'm better, I work hard for a while, but then I start to slip again. I lose my focus. I start spending time on things that don't matter.

What kingdom work are you called to do?

What distractions keep you from doing it?

Main takeaway: Loving well is patiently going the pace you need to go to keep in step with your neighbor, family member, coworker, spouse, etc. We are called to be patient with our loved ones, especially those who are straying. And don't forget how patient God is being with you!

Love Is Kind

In Matthew 5:44 Jesus said, **"Love your enemies and pray for those who persecute you."** In Luke chapter 6, Jesus took it a step further. He told us to be kind to our enemies, lend to them, be merciful to them, serve them, and do good to them. Pastor Mike explained that an enemy is someone who is hostile toward you and persecutes you.

Sometimes I don't want to do this. I can overlook a cranky person, an impatient person, an overzealous person, but be kind to someone who is *hostile* toward me or my family?

Being kind to those who mistreat us is ultimately telling God he is worthy of our trust. He'll sort it all out now, later, or at the final judgment. Since love doesn't allow for holding grudges (see "keeps no record of wrongs"), our job is to be kind and leave the rest up to God.

Being kind will show in our words. When someone makes a poor decision, we could put them down to make them feel stupid. We could remind them of all the times they've made wrong decisions in the past. But that wouldn't be acting the way Jesus acted.

Jesus didn't berate the woman at the well who had been married five times. His very presence was an act of concern. He didn't see her as a throwaway or a screwup or beyond help. She was worthy of his time, and he couldn't wait to tell her he came to bring her salvation.

Even more amazing was the fact that Jesus didn't berate the people who put him on a cross. He could have cried, "Just wait till you realize what you've done!" or, "When you stand before the throne of God, you're going straight to hell!" Instead, Jesus prayed, "Father, forgive them." It's almost unimaginable that Jesus was concerned for the souls of the men who went out of their way to frame him and approved of him being beaten and brutally murdered even though he hadn't done anything but threaten their political power.

Impossible though it may seem to meet someone who harmed us—physically, emotionally, or verbally—with undeserved love and not with anger is to treat them exactly how God deals with us.

Matthew West wrote his song "Forgiveness" after he heard about a woman whose daughter was killed by a drunk driver. When this mother saw the 24-year-old man being sentenced in court, she made it her mission to tell people about the importance of not driving drunk. Years later she realized she hadn't forgiven the man, so she wrote him a letter telling him she forgave him. He wrote back: "I don't know how you can forgive me. I can't even forgive myself." Because of her letter, the young man became a Christian.

But that's only half of the story. This mom went further. She petitioned the judge to reduce the man's sentence from 22 years to 11 years. When he was released, the young man became part of her family.

Chances are likely that you and I will never have the opportunity to do something on that big of a scale. But we might open our home to the person who has put things on social media that criticized or condemned us.

My husband and I had that opportunity not long ago. We had a call from a friend from the past. He was just down the street and wanted to stop by. When I hung up the phone, my husband said, "But, Amber! Look what he posts on Facebook! Look at the things he says!"

Who better to invite into our home? Who better to listen to and offer hospitality? Who better to smother with the same kindness God offers us? Our sinful nature is every bit as hostile to God. Our words and actions align us with Satan as often if not more than our words and actions align us with our Savior. And yet he provides, loves, renews, and forgives.

If you were to list friends and enemies, who would end up in the enemy column?

Make a point in the next week to call that person, invite them to coffee, send them a text. Pray God shows you some way to be kind to them.

One easy way to be kind is to choose our words carefully. Sometimes it's choosing to say nothing at all or changing the tone we use when we do say something.

James said, **"Everyone should be quick to listen, slow to speak and slow to become angry"** (1:19). If only we took an extra minute before answering or a day before responding to an email. If only we adjusted the tone to make sure our words didn't come out like a weapon to cut someone down.

Having children is a wonderful way to keep your tone in check. Not only will children pick up your phraseology, but they will also imitate your tone. If you sneer, they will do it better. If you are sassy, you'll get it back.

I used to pride myself on being the queen of sarcasm. When my children inherited my sarcastic tendencies, it wasn't as funny as I thought. These days I'd rather be kind than get a laugh at the expense of another's feelings. I'd rather build someone up then take a cheap shot that puts them down. I would rather show someone the love of God than have them feel the sting of sin.

Make a point to listen to your words and your tone. With whom and when do the condescending tones appear?

Think of someone who has shown kindness to you. I have a friend who takes my complaints and finds reasons for me to be grateful. She's done it so often that if I start to complain to her, I'm already looking for ways to see God's hand in the situation. Look back at the names you wrote down previously. List something you like about each person. The next time you start to complain about them, remind yourself of that trait.

Our words can affect the people around us, but so can our actions. Think of the note or card you got in the mail during a hard time or something someone did that meant the world to you.

My parents were diagnosed with cancer ten days apart. Both required surgery, and my dad's surgery was extensive. A good friend texted me to let me know she'd be bringing a meal the night before surgery. It would be ready to eat anytime so people could heat up what they wanted whenever they were hungry. It was such a blessing knowing my family was taken care of while I was at the hospital.

Being kind isn't about huge gestures. It's letting someone who is clearly in a bigger hurry than you cut in your lane of traffic. It's telling the person who has two things to go in front of your full cart in the grocery line.

It is comforting the neighbor child who missed the bus and making sure they have a ride to school. It is smiling to strangers and noticing the lonely. It's helping without being asked and keeping your eyes open for ways to be a bright spot in someone's life.

One of the kindest things we can do is pray.

One of the kindest things we can do is pray. The apostle Peter tells us to **"be alert and of sober mind. Your enemy the devil prowls around like a roaring lion looking for someone to devour"** (1 Peter 5:8). Being alert is taking cues from conversations around you. As a person expresses exasperation with their children, worries about money issues, or struggles with family, pray for that person. When you get a chance, remind them you are doing so!

Every conversation leads to prayer. As someone opens up about what's going on in their life, if we're alert, we will know how to pray. Satan is always on the prowl, hoping to take every issue and use it for destruction and despair. We can take the situation to God. If you don't know how to pray about a situation, just invite God to be part of it.

When Jesus told the parable of the sower and the seed, he talked about seed that fell on rocky soil and among thorns. He explained this was like a person who heard the Word and believed it; but when troubles or the worries of this life arrived, the trouble and worry snuffed out the faith of the person in the same way thorns and rocks snuff out a little seedling. The writer of Hebrews said, **"Encourage one another daily . . . so that none of you may be hardened by sin's deceitfulness"** (3:13). Being kind will lead us to notice and encourage those who are struggling.

Whom do you know who is struggling right now?

What little acts of kindness would make their life easier and show them you care?

A friend's husband was good at buying over-the-top gifts for Christmas and her birthday. Once when I was gushing about how amazing his gifts were, she explained she would much rather have a husband who was kind in little things every day than one who made big sweeping gestures twice a year.

Those little gifts or words of appreciation remind people of the value they have in God's eyes. Thanking people for their good work and showing appreciation for a person's efforts can be just what that person needs to keep going. The world is a cruel place. Nasty emails will happen. People will push us aside and ignore us and make us seem invisible in any number of ways.

Our words and actions can reflect the love of Jesus, who loved us enough to leave heaven to experience our struggles firsthand. Our words and actions can be little imitations of God the Father, who works on our behalf day after day to make sure we have what we need. And our words and actions can point to the Holy Spirit who breathed words into men's minds so they could write the Bible so we could see God's plan of salvation and how much we mean to him.

Gary Chapman introduced us to the five love languages. It's especially meaningful when people show us love with the love language *we* prefer. Unfortunately, we usually give others the love language we prefer. To go out of our way to do acts of service or give words of affirmation, physical touch, gifts, or quality time, even when that isn't our preferred love language, will make an impact on others.

Do you know what love language the people closest to you desire? What can you do to make sure they feel loved and appreciated?

Think of someone outside your normal circle of friends who might appreciate a little something this week. What can you do to encourage them and make sure they feel loved?

Main takeaway: Ultimately, Jesus was 100% truth, but he was also 100% grace. He didn't shy away from the truth, but as Pastor Mike pointed out, his criticism or his toughness was tempered with tenderness. There will be times we need to be tough, but our tenderness and our kindness should be the difference between us and the rest of the world.

Love Does Not Envy

If you were to look at the highlight reel from the biblical lives of Sarah, Joseph, Daniel, and Esther, you might become envious.

Sarah was married to a prominent and wealthy man. She is one of only a few women in the Bible who is described as beautiful. Her husband had a deep connection to God, and God spoke to him and told him what to do.

Joseph was good-looking, could interpret dreams, and became second-in-command of Egypt.

Daniel was intelligent, good-looking, could interpret dreams, and became a high official to Nebuchadnezzar the ruler of the Babylonian empire.

Esther was described as "lovely in form and features" and was chosen out of all the young women in the land to be queen to Xerxes, king of Persia.

In comparison, your life might not look so interesting.

A closer look at these four people's lives would reveal a different picture.

Sarah desperately wanted a child. In fact, God promised Abraham that he would be the father of many, but Abraham and Sarah waited 25 long years after the promise for it to happen. In an attempt to aid God in this plan, Abraham conceived a child with Sarah's servant, bringing turmoil and plenty of frustrations to their lives.

Joseph was sold by his brothers who hated him. It was plan B. Plan A was to kill him. He was taken from his homeland and sold into slavery, then falsely accused of attempted rape, and put in prison.

Daniel was taken captive, taken away from his family

and homeland and made to live in a foreign land where idolatry was status quo. His resolute desire to serve God often put him and his friends at odds with everyone else. This was a lifelong challenge, and he ended up in a lions' den at an age most of us would consider elderly.

Esther was orphaned. When both her father and mother were killed, she was raised by her cousin Mordecai. She, and all the other young, beautiful virgins, were confiscated by Xerxes, brought to the king in the evening to be tried out, and then sent away to await her fate.

A true picture of these lives shows heartache, separation, strife, infertility, and no say in the direction their lives went.

Love doesn't envy, in part because as we walk with the Lord, we recognize anytime we look longingly at someone else's life, we're only seeing part of the picture. To want what someone else has without fully understanding all the implications of that desire is foolish.

There's a saying that goes something like this: If everyone were to put their problems in a pile in front of them, you'd likely keep yours.

Our time is better spent working on our lives instead of longing for someone else's. Do what you can to deal with the problems you face. Pray and ask for God's help. Focus on where you and your family are going and what they are doing, rather than wishing for a different scenario.

List your three biggest worries/problems:

_____

_____

_____

Now write down something tangible you can do to eliminate each issue. If eliminating the problem isn't feasible, write down the things you'll pray for to get you through.

It's easy to become envious when you look at the talents and abilities God gives to others, and it's easy to be envious of someone else's spiritual gifts too. I have a friend who excels at hospitality. Her house looks like something straight out of *Better Homes and Gardens*. She has table décor for every season, and when you're a guest at her house, you'll have a large assortment of food and drinks to choose from.

It's silly for me to waste time bemoaning that I haven't been given that gift because by design God gifts us all uniquely. Some are encouragers, some are administrators, some excel at teaching. The apostle Paul said, **"For just as each of us has one body with many members, and these members do not all have the same function, so in Christ we, though many, form one body, and each member belongs to all the others. We have different gifts, according to the grace given to each of us. If your gift is prophesying, then prophesy in accordance with your faith; if it is serving, then serve; if it is teaching, then teach; if it is to encourage, then give encouragement; if it is giving, then give generously; if it is to lead, do it diligently; if it is to show mercy, do it cheerfully"** (Romans 12:4-8).

Whatever gifts you have received are for you to use in God's kingdom to build up those in the kingdom and to bring others in. If God didn't gift you specifically in one way, it was because he gifted you to do something else. Whatever the Spirit gave you was intentional. He knew where and when you would live and what the believers around you would need. (For a great Time of Grace resource on this topic, check out Dr. Bruce Becker's book *Gifted for More*.)

Envy is easy enough to fall into, but it isn't from God. Envy is another tool the devil uses to keep us from doing what God would have us do. If I think about how awesome your gift is, I get depressed and do nothing. I'd rather focus on my gift and use it to its full potential.

God doesn't make us compete with each other to see who can do more. The only measure of our performance is if we used what God gave us to use.

If you are an encourager, have you encouraged others? Can you send a text, an email, a card to lift another up? If you can teach, who are you teaching? If you are gifted to show mercy, who have you been helping?

Main takeaway: Envy will keep you from the important work God has for you to do. Pastor Mike's reminder is one to keep close: Christian love does not want a monopoly on God's blessing. Christian love will cheer one another on and build one another up and rejoice at the ways God blesses all his children.

Love Does Not Boast, Is Not Proud

A dear friend taught me a wonderful lesson in humility. We were both working at a particular place, and one of our coworkers made a pretty significant blunder. As we were talking about it, my friend said, "I didn't screw up this time, but that's not to say it won't be me to screw up the next time." That was a pretty significant lesson to me. Instead of kicking this person when she was down, my friend humbly recognized we're all capable of mistakes.

Pride insists on coming out on top. Pride will justify every action, make sure to have the last word, and put another down to make sure I am number one. If it doesn't sound fun to be around, it's because it's not. If those police officers at the protest Pastor Mike happened upon had been proud, they would have watched aloofly from afar, instead of leaving their post to dance. Pride will keep us a safe distance from others too.

A humble person isn't afraid to be around someone who's screwed up. Jesus went to a tax collector's house when it was taboo to be around tax collectors. He stayed behind to meet the woman at the well. Even though he came from heaven and had never screwed up anything, Jesus wasn't afraid to be around those who had.

Probably the easiest place to boast right now is on social media. If you are your ideal weight, let the world know. When your hair looks good, post a picture. When the family is on vacation or all together for a holiday, look at us! When your child gets a medal for his sport, when she comes in first at the spelling bee, when she's a starter and having a great season, post it and wait for the praise to come in.

There's nothing that stings quite as much as seeing the pictures of people succeeding when you are barely putting one foot in front of the other. It's painful to see the pictures of your friend's children on the team when your child got cut. Seeing everyone else's family smiling and enjoying a holiday makes it that much more apparent when you're alone.

That's not to say all social media is bad. It's just to say it is a place where boasting is easy and acceptable.

I noticed a long time ago, as did many of you, that social media is a false narrative. It is us telling a story using only the dialogue and pictures we want others to see. The smiling faces of the family on vacation don't attest to the squabbling among children ten minutes prior. The elation doesn't recount the hours waiting in lines in the heat or the moment your children found a couch near the bathrooms and refused to get up for 45 minutes. The senior pictures are a snapshot, the glowing grad with the things they love most, but that picture doesn't portray the classes your child barely passed or the hours spent arguing about how pointless a class was.

And yet many of us spend so much of our day scrolling and scrolling and scrolling. And when we leave social media, more often than not, we feel significantly "less than" other people.

Do you lean more toward the "got to post the highlight reel" or the "get sucked into feeling bad looking at everyone else's life" camp?

Whom do you love to follow on social media and why?

So how can we avoid being a boaster on social media platforms or falling into the "my life stinks because I'm seeing everyone else's highlights" whirlwind? It may sound obvious, but to avoid boasting, we might start by turning social media off. It might not only help us avoid boasting, but it might help us avoid envying those who seem to have it all together.

During the lockdowns of 2020, my husband and I did quite a few landscaping and house projects. Because we had a graduate the next year, our projects continued into 2021. That may sound ambitious or pretentious, but I can assure you it was nothing more than us trying to catch up from years and years and years of neglecting the maintenance and attention we probably should have been putting into our house. It mostly meant going through a lot of stuff and getting rid of half of what we'd accumulated, taking the junk that was cluttering our house to the dump, and getting a very unkempt yard somewhat under control. None of the before and after pics made it onto social media. The before pics would have brought embarrassment, and afterward we were exhausted and just grateful to have things finished.

When I limited my time on social media to only a few minutes a day, I realized my to-do list was more than enough to keep me occupied. And I'm far happier working on my stuff than I am when I'm sitting and looking at someone else's life. Now, thanks to the cleanup, we've opened our home and deck to others often. Time spent with others is much better than cuddling on the couch wishing I was partaking of half of what others were doing.

How much time do you spend on social media a day?

What project(s) need your attention, or what could you do if you cut that number down?

Too often blind devotion to political parties and sports figures or teams, a media outlet, or celebrities leads to boasting and puts us at odds with our neighbors and community members. It's silly, really, because so much of what happens politically, or on the field or floor, has nothing to do with us. We take credit for cheering them on, but we're not out there making a good catch. We act superior if our candidate wins, but how often hasn't a scandal two, three, or four years later shown the politician we voted for isn't who we thought he or she was? Our boasts are grounded in the narrative the politician or coach or media outlet gives us, which may or may not have anything to do with the truth.

Still, we show up in the jersey and on the couch glued to the TV. We put the bumper sticker on the car, and when given the opportunity, we defend and boast.

James' said, "Now listen, you who say, 'Today or tomorrow we will go to this or that city, spend a year there, carry on business and make money.' Why, you do not even know what will happen tomorrow. What is your life? You are a mist that appears for a little while and then vanishes. Instead, you ought to say, 'If it is the Lord's will, we will live and do this or that'" (4:13-15).

We boast about things we don't know or have any means to predict. The world cheers for points and goals and wins. It applauds the digs, the trips, the foul, and the one-liner that destroyed the opponent. It doesn't cheer for character growth or standing for the truth.

What sports team or musician or politician have you been devoted to?

Do you have the same devotion for Jesus and his church? Why or why not?

While the world doesn't cheer for humility, it is one of the two words Jesus used to describe himself. He said, "Come to me, all you who are weary . . . for I am gentle and humble . . . and you will find rest" (Matthew 11:28,29). I haven't read Dane Ortlund's book *Gentle and Lowly* that Pastor Mike mentioned in a previous chapter, but as of this writing, it has over six thousand positive reviews on Amazon. And I think it may be because a proud person won't comfort you when you're down, but a humble person will. It can be hard to find people like my friend who humbly admit, even if they didn't screw up this time, they have plenty of times before and likely will at some point in the future. When humility is hard to find, there's Jesus. He's the one person who has more reason than the rest of us to be proud and arrogant, but he embraced humility and welcomes us because of it.

Main takeaway: Instead of posting your pictures on social media, consider taking a minute to thank the Lord for whatever it was you were about to share. Pray for others who are struggling in that area. Carefully consider your devotion to people you don't personally know and be devoted to Jesus above all!

Love Does Not Dishonor Others

It's easy enough to dishonor someone. Just talk over them as if their words don't matter. Tell them the suggestion is good to their face but never follow through. Find someone else who knows them and talk about them, naming all the faults and reasons you've carefully gathered for why they aren't worthy of your respect.

Those are overt, and maybe not something you often see. Christians often fall into the same sort of thing, only in subtle ways. First, there's the "I need to tell you so you can pray" excuse. It comes in a phone call, an email, a text, once in a while in a message. "So and so did such and such. Pray!"

Before you get too upset, I need to be clear. Collective prayer is powerful and godly. That's not what I'm talking about. Most of us routinely ask for prayers from friends and brothers and sisters in Christ. That is us telling our news to the people we want to hear it.

It's a totally different thing to spread gossip under the guise of a prayer request. I'm guessing most, if not all, of us have done it. We've all witnessed it. Some things seem too good to keep to ourselves.

One section of Scripture consistently comes to mind when I get those messages:

> Is anyone among you in trouble? Let them pray. Is anyone happy? Let them sing songs of praise. Is anyone among you sick? Let them call the elders of the church to pray over them and anoint them with oil in the name of the Lord. And the prayer offered in faith will make the sick person well; the Lord will raise them up.

If they have sinned, they will be forgiven. Therefore confess your sins to each other and pray for each other so that you may be healed. The prayer of a righteous person is powerful and effective.

Elijah was a human being, even as we are. He prayed earnestly that it would not rain, and it did not rain on the land for three and a half years. Again he prayed, and the heavens gave rain, and the earth produced its crops. (James 5:13-18)

Here we learn the power of one. One person praying is powerful and effective.

Pastor Jeremy Mattek, in his *Time of Grace* TV message titled "Your Prayers Can Be Powerful," said, "Prayer is the privilege of being able to use the resources of heaven to change this world's direction. And who is it that God entrusts with the resources of heaven? That passage from James says the prayer of the righteous person is powerful and effective."

In the book of Hebrews, we learn a little more. We're told, **"Without faith it is impossible to please God, because anyone who comes to him must believe that he exists and that he rewards those who earnestly seek him"** (11:6).

We become righteous through faith in Jesus. When we pray, we must pray to the triune God, or we're just praying to an idol. If we pray to the universe or mother nature or the old man upstairs or to one of our deceased relatives, we shouldn't expect an answer. We must also believe our prayers are not in vain. They go before the throne of God. Even if we don't see the answer immediately or if we don't get the answer we want, we know our prayers are heard.

And that's why it's not necessary to call everyone and

their uncle to let them know what someone has done or that the cancer has spread or that he was actually drinking when the accident occurred.

God is able to answer the prayer of one. When you know sensitive information, ask yourself, Would the person this information is about want me to tell others? If you're not sure how they would respond, then pray and keep the news to yourself, knowing God is able to answer the prayer of one.

Think of a time someone shared information about you that you didn't want shared. How did that impact your relationship?

Sometimes telling someone else is a matter of taking the pressure off. If I tell someone, then they'll pray, and if I forget, I won't feel bad. What can you do to make sure you remember to pray for the people who ask you to pray?

Telling other's shortcomings and secrets dishonors those around us, but so does ignoring their concerns. And it is so easy to do! When a child comes in with what seems to be a minor complaint, it's easy to dismiss. But the complaint isn't minor to that child! When my children were young, it was easy to get caught up in all the things they needed. Once in a while, I needed to tell the children to stop, wait, or hold on for a bit so I could focus on my husband. Sometimes Grandma's to-do list takes a back seat for way too many months before we all get together to help out.

It's easy for it to happen in organizations too. The head elder's concerns should be taken every bit as seriously as the widow's or the organist's or even the teen who shows up once a month. Sometimes called workers are given more leniency than members of the congregation or rules are enforced in certain families but not in others.

James instructs us again. He said, **"If you really keep the royal law found in Scripture, 'Love your neighbor as yourself,' you are doing right. But if you show favoritism, you sin and are convicted by the law as lawbreakers"** (2:8,9).

If we aren't careful, it can be common to hear these complaints in our homes: "You always listen to your coworkers but never listen to me. You make time to fix the neighbor's problem or help that person out, but I seem to end up at the end of your list. Why are you so nice to so and so but mean to me?"

Do any of those sound familiar? Regretfully, I think most of us have heard some version of those complaints.

Jesus championed noticing the unnoticeable. He not only noticed the tax collectors; he hung out with them. He made a deliberate stop to talk to the swindler glancing at him from up in a tree (Luke 19). The religious leaders took issue with the fact that Jesus ate with the unmentionables of society (Matthew 9:11).

Society deems many people as unworthy of our time and energy. The elderly are often overlooked. In my years working as an elderly companion, I find the time I spend with the elderly to be a blessing. My life is enriched by the stories I hear and the advice I am given.

Sometimes being noticed is the only love a person gets all day. That person walking down the street may be going home to a dark house. The person in line at the store may be divorced or widowed, and his children may live far away. Loving like Jesus is the little reminder we can give others that Jesus loves them.

You can't do it all. You can't work 16-hour days for the high-paying job and take care of your aging mother and be a father and a husband. You might not be able to have meaningful conversations with your spouse, help your children or grandchildren with their homework, and get to all your emails.

Aligning your values with God's is not likely to put you in the spotlight of society. The world's ideals and God's are very different.

Think through a typical week. Whom do you routinely dismiss and why?

How would your relationship change if you took time to listen to that person?

Honoring others may mean making them the priority they should be. Look up Lauren Daigle's song "First" that Pastor Mike mentioned. When God is in his rightful place, we'll be more likely to keep the people in our lives in the place God would have them be.

And the best motivator is remembering that God always makes time for us. He is never too busy, never tells us to come back later because heaven is closed. We can pray anytime.

Main takeaway: Pay special attention to how you talk about others. Are you honoring others by what you choose to say or not say about someone else? If you're anything like me, I need to reorder my priorities every so often so the people in my life don't get the short end of the stick. Taking care of others honors the person, and it also honors God.

Love Is Not Self-Seeking

Pastor Mike explained that so many of our frustrations and disagreements happen because what gets first priority in our lives puts "me" at odds with "your" priorities. For young Mike that resulted in a turf war between him and his roller hockey-loving friends and the neighbor with the manicured lawn.

What would it take for you to reprioritize your life? For me it was the suicide of my neighbor. We had done so much life together. My husband and I bought property from his family. I took care of his aging father. We shoveled each other's drives and took in each other's mail. We met on the boulevard and waved and discussed how messed up the world was.

I had been on his deck chatting with his wife four hours before she found him dead. I had seen him mow the lawn that afternoon while I was working in my yard just a stone's throw away. I didn't go to the property line and wave or take the few steps from the deck into the living room where he was sitting. I didn't go out of my way to say hello or ask how he was doing because I didn't know he'd be gone in a few hours.

When chatting with his bereaved daughter a few days later, I repented. Why was I so caught up in my lawn? Why was I so engrossed in my own discussion to notice a mentally broken friend 10 feet away on the other side of the door?

That night my priorities changed dramatically. Too often I've ignored my children while working on a project. I've spent days and weeks on house projects or lawn projects when I could have been investing in people. I get caught up in my life and entertainment at the expense of time in prayer or reaching out to the lost and broken.

I am not easily jarred out of self-centeredness. It took a global pandemic for me to slow down, go through my house, and get it to the point where I was comfortable letting people in the door any time they showed up on my doorstep. Prior to that we filled our calendar so full that we were barely home long enough to drop our things and regroup prior to leaving again. Clutter collected on every open space. It took major holidays to clean it, and within a few weeks we were back to piles and hoping and praying no one knocked on the door.

Look at your calendar. Make a list of your current priorities based on how you spend your time.

Is it the way you want to be spending your time? If not, what would you like to be doing that you aren't?

Time is one of the gifts we are given to steward, along with our energy, talents, and finances. It's easy to fall into greed in any one of these aspects. Where do you spend your energy? What do you do with extra income when it comes?

I don't think we deliberately set out to be self-centered. Most of us fall into it by not being deliberate about avoiding it. One way to escape self-centeredness is using Jesus' words in the Garden of Gethsemane. He prayed, "Not my will, but yours."

Imagine if that became part of our daily prayers. How long would it take for God to break us of self-centered habits? And if we pray God helps us notice others and their needs, we can be sure he will open our eyes.

Jesus was in tune to those others ignored. Remember the blind man shouting, **"Jesus, Son of David, have mercy on me!"** (Luke 18:38)? People were rebuking the man and telling him to be quiet. Jesus went to the man and healed him.

If Jesus was concerned with being popular or making worldly alliances, he wouldn't have taken the time to stop in front of a blind beggar. People, especially the downtrodden, *were* his agenda. Over and over Jesus showed that God's grace isn't just for those of worldly status. In fact, you might say the only people Jesus routinely avoided were those of political and religious power.

Every miracle Jesus did was for the benefit of someone else. If he was self-seeking, he would have turned the stones into bread as Satan suggested. He would have sought power and honor and glory and used his power to do so. He didn't. He stayed in lonely places. He experienced fatigue and hunger. And still, he looked out for others. In Matthew chapter 15, Jesus had compassion on the people who had been with him for three days. He knew if they set out for home, some of them would collapse on the road. So he fed them.

That is extraordinary compassion. Oh, God, give me the same kind of heart!

If you had all the time and money you needed, whom would you want to help?

What might you need to stop doing today in order to make that happen?

The one thing everyone needs is a relationship with God. When our time on earth is over, it won't matter what we had or didn't have or who was or wasn't our friend. Our relationship with Jesus will determine our place for eternity.

We have the answer everyone needs. Are we concerned with the people in our neighborhood, the people we work with, the people we see in our community? Or are we content that we are saved and that's all that matters?

The one thing everyone needs is a relationship with God.

The apostle Paul traveled, not because he wanted to see the world but because he knew what it was to be lost. Once he understood who Jesus was, he wanted everyone else to know too. What if that was our motivator? What if that shaped where we worked, how we spent our time, where we spent our money?

Too often my decisions are based on what is convenient, beneficial, and comfortable for me and my family, not on evangelism or how I can reach the most people with the Word of God. My prayers are mostly about my family, my friends, and my relatives. Clearly I am not grieved enough about the lost, or it would occupy more of my time and dominate my prayers.

This too comes down to being self-centered and seeking what makes me happy and comfortable to feel as if I'm in control. Only God can light the fire and fan into flame a desire to spread his Word. It's what happened on Pentecost, not long after Jesus ascended. Prior to that day the disciples were huddled together, too scared to be seen in public. If their leader was killed, what would stop anyone from crucifying them?

But when the Spirit came on them, everything changed.

They spoke fearlessly to the crowd and went out day after day after day to spread the good news.

We have access to the same Spirit, but too often we put out the flame. We keep our Bibles shut and forget to pray. We half-heartedly go to church and daydream through the sermon. We listen to self-help or entrepreneur podcasts and with the remainder of our day entertain ourselves into contentment.

Thank God for the things that shake us out of complacency and move us to care for lost souls. And thank God for the illnesses that put us in the hospital and clinical setting next to other people looking for peace. And thank God for the wake-up calls that bring us to the jails to see the lost and confused people.

If we all started praying for a heart eager to share Jesus and opportunities to spread his Word, we might be surprised at how different our lives would look.

In what areas have you become comfortable? What can't you imagine leaving (your house, your job, your city)?

Are you willing to pray for God to use you, even if it takes you to uncomfortable places?

What area of ministry have you considered but never gotten around to doing? Is it time to make it a priority?

Main takeaway: Our priorities show where our hearts are. It's so easy to get caught up in our lives. Jesus never succumbed to that pressure. He sought out the people society ignored. With God's help, we can do the same.

Love Is Not Easily Angered

I can be extraordinarily patient with some things, and other things send me through the roof almost immediately. Why? Three reasons: 1) Because the hurt experienced from such things in the past have whittled down my tolerance of them; 2) blind rage convinces me these things are unacceptable and everyone should see it; and 3) pride keeps me from recognizing my shortcomings and instead focuses on the shortcomings of others. In order not to fly off the handle, two things need to occur. First, I need to be aware of the three aforementioned things above; second, I need good friends and family to keep me accountable.

What things tend to lead you to anger? Is it your impatience with people who don't drive the way you do or a slow cashier? Do you lose your temper with a spouse who wakes you up on your day off or a neighbor who plays their music too loud?

Look at that list from the standpoint of blessings. If you become irritated with drivers, it is because you have a car, a means of getting from point A to B. If you are waiting for a cashier, it is because you have access to food, something many in the world do not have. If you have a spouse who wakes you up, you have someone to share your life with. And that neighbor who plays their music too loud means you aren't in prison and you can hear. What blessings do you see in the things that make you angry?

When I'm thinking rationally, I recognize it's not fair to the person I'm angry with that I'm reacting because of my past hurts. How should they know what has caused my pain? There's no way they could. The problem of course is that I don't always think rationally.

If I had an ex-boyfriend who snuck around and I found out he was cheating, I probably wouldn't be very tolerant of someone who isn't immediately forthcoming with their whereabouts. If I was belittled as a child, I may writhe at the slightest hint of condescension, even if I'm reading into what wasn't there in an email. If I've been overlooked for job opportunities in the past, I might read into a delayed response to a text or email as being overlooked again.

What past hurts have you experienced that have manifested into intolerance?

_____

_____

_____

_____

_____

_____

_____

_____

_____

_____

    Self-awareness is key in this situation! Once we realize what causes our anger, we can work to control it. When anger strikes, stop. Take a breath. Remember it isn't this person's fault that you are sensitive to this issue. Say a quick prayer.

    Sometimes our expectations are out of whack. We expect the secular world to treat people the way God tells us to treat people. We expect our children to know all we know. We expect new Christians to be more spiritually mature than they are. We expect the elderly to understand, keep up, do things our way.

    Sometimes we have reason to be disappointed when our expectations aren't met. A wayward child can cause serious frustration for Christian parents. But does anger help?

Which unmet expectations have led you to anger lately?

Were your expectations unreasonable, or were you disappointed in the lack of effort from someone else?

I get a lot further with my older children when I express my frustrations minus the anger and edginess. When my tone is even-tempered and unemotional, my young adults are much more likely to hear what I say. Too often anger sabotages my effort and leads to less communication and understanding.

Pride leads me to think I'm more important than others. I used to get annoyed with other drivers on the road when I was in a hurry to get to work. One day I realized they were not the problem. The problem was that I left with just enough time to get to work if every light was green. That is a silly assumption to make. I had to go through the heart of downtown to get to work, so the probability that I wouldn't need to stop was almost zero. Once I started leaving for work five minutes earlier, I rarely became annoyed.

A selfish, self-centered worldview will have us looking at every situation only from the standpoint of how the situation affects me. The apostle Paul said, **"Do nothing out of selfish ambition or vain conceit. Rather, in humility value others above yourselves, not looking to your own interests but each of you to the interests of the others"** (Philippians 2:3,4).

Pride looks only at me. "Why can't they do what is best for me? Why don't they give me what I want? Why can't I do what I want? Why can't they see it my way?"

Humility considers and looks out for the interests of others. "If I do this, how will it impact them? Would my actions hurt the other person or inconvenience them? How can I do the most good in this situation? How can I serve God and others well?"

When you're slipping into anger, ask yourself, "Do I feel

this way because I'm not getting my way? If I saw it from the other person's perspective, would I feel differently?"

Go back to the things that routinely make you angry. How would considering the other person change your focus?

I've found one of the greatest deterrents to becoming prideful is remembering how God feels about pride. James 4:6 reminds us, **"God opposes the proud but shows favor to the humble."** I don't want to be God's opposition. I want to be on the receiving end of God's favor. C. S. Lewis said, "True humility is not thinking less of yourself; it's thinking of yourself less." Or, as Pastor Mike likes to say, "You first."

After receiving an email addressed to me and a friend,

I sent the friend a text complaining and asking, "Why do I even try?" The friend replied by recognizing how frustrated I must be and suggesting I hang in there and keep working hard, even if my efforts aren't immediately understood or appreciated. Because of that text, I did not respond to the email with the scathing response I otherwise might have. Instead, I waited two full days. When my anger subsided, I presented my case for moving forward. The reward of waiting was immediately apparent as my email was met with approval.

Naaman was a commander in the king of Aram's army. He had prestige and wealth and, unfortunately, leprosy. When a servant girl directed him to the prophet in Israel for healing, he set off with a great entourage. Elisha didn't give Naaman the satisfaction of swooning over his glitz and glamor. He didn't go out to meet him but sent his servant with instructions: **"Go, wash yourself seven times in the Jordan, and your flesh will be restored and you will be cleansed"** (2 Kings 5:10).

You might think Naaman did a happy dance. His request was granted, and all he had to do was dunk himself in a river. But that's not what happened.

> But Naaman went away angry and said, "I thought that he would surely come out to me and stand and call on the name of the Lord his God, wave his hand over the spot and cure me of my leprosy. Are not Abana and Pharpar, the rivers of Damascus, better than all the waters of Israel? Couldn't I wash in them and be cleansed?" So, he turned and went off in a rage.
>
> Naaman's servants went to him and said, "My father, if the prophet had told you to do some great thing,

would you not have done it? How much more, then, when he tells you, 'Wash and be cleansed'!" So he went down and dipped himself in the Jordan seven times, as the man of God had told him, and his flesh was restored and became clean like that of a young boy.** (2 Kings 5:10-14)

We all need friends like Naaman's servants. Naaman's pride would have kept him from being healed. His anger would have disregarded the small act of faith God would use to change his life. If you don't have someone in your life who can walk you off the anger cliff, start praying God gives you that person right now. If you do have that friend or family member, thank God and be sure to thank the person too.

Are you the voice who calms someone down when they call or text because they are ready to blow up? Or do you tend to fuel the fire? Naaman's servants could have said, "This is stupid. How dare he tell you to do this? You don't have to put up with this." And that would have been the end of it. They would have gone back to their homeland, and Naaman would have died a leper.

Main takeaway: Sometimes experiences from our past cause us to respond in anger to situations. It's important to understand this about ourselves so we don't release undue rage on an unsuspecting friend or acquaintance. Unmet expectations can lead to all kinds of grief if we don't put all situations in God's hands. And unchecked pride causes not only anger but might keep us from situations and people who would be a blessing.

Love Keeps No Record of Wrongs

I still remember the popular girl in elementary school, the one everyone wanted to sit by at lunch and hang out with after school. I remember many things about her, not the least of which was that you didn't want to make her mad. If you did, you knew you would get the silent treatment for days.

Most of us are pretty good scorekeepers. Sometimes we fall into this in our homes or workplaces. When your spouse does "that" again, you bring it up. When your son or daughter falls into the same pattern, you immediately start to nag. When your coworker drinks the coffee but never contributes toward buying more, you take note.

My children, and all their friends, know that I have two rules. One, no one blocks the driveway. Since three of my four kids drive and have friends visiting often, this can be a serious issue. The second rule is curfew is midnight unless you have spoken to my husband or me prior. That rule hasn't been very popular with my older kids. Recently one of my older children was explaining why they arrived home an hour and a half late. Their car was acting up, and they had two friends to drop off. They came home, switched cars, and took said friends home.

I started to interrupt to question a choice, and this child said, "Mom, can you just praise my decision-making in the situation?"

After a few seconds, I said, "Fair enough. Given the situation, your decisions kept everyone safe, and I'm glad of that."

Sometimes I'm guilty of making mountains out of molehills. Maybe, just maybe, you do the same.

Take a good look at the people you spend the most time with (your family, the people in the apartment next door, your coworkers). Who are you most likely to get into nag mode with and for what offenses?

When you look back on your life, are these offenses ones you will be glad you held on to?

Some things are worth fighting for. Others may not be. Are these things worth the energy and expense of the relationship to keep fighting about?

Some of us struggle, not so much with our children or our spouse, but with "those people." You remember what your neighbor did two summers ago and the comment your in-law made. There's a reason you don't serve on that committee at church anymore.

Very few of us are God-like in this capacity. In Isaiah 43:25, God says, **"I, even I, am he who blots out your transgressions, for my own sake, and remembers your sins no more."**

You might argue that only holds true for Christians, right? So even God treats others differently.

In Paul's first letter to Timothy, he wrote, **"I urge, then, first of all, that petitions, prayers, intercession and thanksgiving be made for all people—for kings and all those in authority, that we may live peaceful and quiet lives in all godliness and holiness. This is good, and pleases God our Savior, who wants all people to be saved and to come to a knowledge of the truth"** (2:1-4).

Jesus bore our sin and the sin of the whole world,

including the neighbor who threatened to sue, the in-law who's never seen you as good enough, even the person at church who just didn't see things your way.

God doesn't treat us as our sins deserve. **"He causes his sun to rise on the evil and the good, and sends rain on the righteous and the unrighteous"** (Matthew 5:45). Or, if you remember Pastor Mike's analogy, the atheist and the churchgoer see the same thing when they pull out their weather apps.

Becoming people who love in such a way as to keep no record of wrongs starts with recognizing our own depravity and God's willingness to blot it out. If God operated the way we so often do, we might wake up to find our own yard woefully dark, while our neighbor, who behaved considerably better the day before, was enjoying sunshine.

What pet sins do you routinely commit? Do you struggle to tell the truth? Do you gossip? Are you prone to lust, overeating, or drinking? Take some time to really examine your life, and be brave and admit those sins below.

_____

_____

_____

_____

_____

_____

I don't know anyone who doesn't have some skeletons in their past, things they are profoundly ashamed of and wish they could forget or undo. They include the times you said something sooooo wrong, the inappropriate behavior with the wrong person, the times you punished your children in anger instead of love.

Now consider the freedom you feel knowing every sin you ever committed is forgiven. God doesn't remember it, and he doesn't want you to dwell on it either. He's taken it away and wiped the slate clean. Amazing, right?

That same freedom is ours when we quit keeping track of other people's sins, because being a scorekeeper is a job. We become burden bearers. Holding on to what our neighbor did is like putting a book in a backpack we have to carry. And when we remember the cruel words of the in-law, that's another book. The things that were said and done in the church meeting, another book.

We keep those grievances near so when we see the neighbor walking down the street, we can reach in the backpack and cling to the book. We wouldn't dream of smiling or waving because that might make it appear we had forgotten their heinous behavior.

There's just one problem. The backpack gets heavy. We live with imperfect people, so day after day we'll need to carry more books. That post on Facebook took a shot at you. Add a book. You heard what someone said behind your back. Add a book.

Wouldn't it be easier and a whole lot more enjoyable to ditch the backpack? Smile and wave at the neighbor. God has forgiven you, and now you can forgive her. Send a nice note to the person who took a shot at you with the Facebook post. Make sure to take the time to catch up with the person who's been talking behind your back. Reconciliation will likely bless you as much or more than it blesses the other person.

A few months back a neighbor girl quit coming over to our house. After some time, I asked my girls what happened. According to them, when the girl got into trouble, she lied to her parents and blamed her bad behavior on my children. In response, her parents said our house was off limits from then on.

Fast-forward several months. I was walking the neighborhood as I do every night and saw the girl's mom outside. I had a choice. I could sneak past and let the awkwardness of the situation continue, or I could slow down, pause, and say hello. Do you know what happened? When I stopped and greeted her, it didn't take two minutes and we were talking like the old friends we were. That's one more person I don't have to worry about seeing in public. Whatever the situation was, and whatever the truth was, one step toward making amends took place.

This is so important to God that he'd rather you mend relationships than give your offering at church. Jesus said, **"If you are offering your gift at the altar and there remember that your brother or sister has something against you, leave your gift there in front of the altar. First go and be reconciled to them; then come and offer your gift"** (Matthew 5:23,24).

Make a list of those you've struggled to get along with in the past months or year and the grievance you are still holding on to.

_____

_____

_____

Now, pray God would soften your heart to forgive the offenses. If you've contributed to the chaos, pray to recognize your role. Then take action—call those people, send a text, stop at their houses, or invite them to yours. Be like those people Pastor Mike talked about at the protest in his city. Invite the other side to dance, and if you are the other side, be like those two uncoordinated but enthusiastic police officers who left the sidelines to dance when invited.

Main takeaway: Satan loves to divide. He wants nothing more than to have hate fester and relationships break down. Every time you choose love instead of hate, you defy Satan and acknowledge that God's way is best. Ditch the scorekeeping backpack and live in the freedom God intended.

Love Does Not Delight in Evil

If you've read the book of Proverbs, you know just how much God hates evil. He is equally bothered by those who delight in participating in evil. Here are just a few verses to illustrate the point.

Proverbs 15:26, "The Lord detests the thoughts of the wicked, but gracious words are pure in his sight."

Proverbs 17:15, "Acquitting the guilty and condemning the innocent—the Lord detests them both."

Proverbs 20:10, "Differing weights and differing measures—the Lord detests them both."

God doesn't pull any punches. He uses strong words. He does not delight in evil. He doesn't want us too either. The flip side of that is to live with integrity. Several people in the Bible serve as excellent examples.

He does not delight in evil.

In Genesis chapter 39 we're told: "Now Joseph was well-built and handsome, and after a while his master's wife took notice of Joseph and said, 'Come to bed with me!' But he refused. 'With me in charge,' he told her, 'my master does not concern himself with anything in the house; everything he owns he has entrusted to my care. No one is greater in this house than I am. My master has withheld nothing from me except you, because you are his wife. How then could I do such a wicked thing and sin against God?' And though she spoke to Joseph day after day, he refused to go to bed with her or even be with her" (6-10).

Joseph recognized the temptation, announced he wouldn't participate in the temptation because he respected his master and God, and took action to make sure he wasn't around her. To put it simply, he resolved to follow God and took action to ensure he wasn't willingly in a place of temptation.

Too often we do just the opposite. How often hasn't season 1 of a series been funny and action-packed and interesting and PG, but season 2 or for sure season 3 was rated R or worse? Did you, like Joseph, remove yourself from the situation to avoid temptation, or did you keep watching because you were invested in the characters and the story line? For me the answer too often has unfortunately been the latter.

Or that amazing new song with the unbelievable beat and mesmerizing lyrics that everyone is singing comes on the radio, and you KNOW the lyrics are irreverent or downright appalling, but you still turn it up and dance along. The opportunity to take a stand for integrity and godliness presented itself and went unnoticed.

Joseph shows us a better way. Don't dabble with temptation or see how far you can go before you fall into sin or stand and watch temptation. Immediately upon realizing Potiphar's wife was interested, Joseph determined not to go to bed with her or even be alone with her.

Think of the temptations you've faced this week. What are you doing to avoid falling into those sins?

Who can you ask to help you stay on track so you don't sin?

When Job's friends accused Job of sinning and causing the grief he was going through, Job defended himself, saying, **"I made a covenant with my eyes not to look lustfully at a young woman. For what is our lot from God above, our heritage from the Almighty on high? Is it not ruin for the wicked, disaster for those who do wrong? Does he not see my ways and count my every step? If I have walked with falsehood or my foot has hurried after deceit—let God weigh me in honest scales and he will know that I am blameless"** (Job 31:1-6).

Knowing his way was in perfect view of the Lord, Job decided to live in such a way as to bring honor to God. He defended his reputation because he made a conscientious choice every day to stand apart.

Would we be so quick to defend ourselves if our reputation was in question, or would we admit we hadn't put good boundaries in place and there was more than enough evidence to convict?

Joseph responded with godliness when temptation occurred. Job was intentional and anticipated temptation before experiencing it. It's somewhat easy to stay sexually pure in middle school but considerably harder in high school or college when you are independent and not always under the watchful eye of an adult. It's probably easier for a retiree with all kinds of time to be patient with a slow cashier than the working mom who stopped at the store for one item so she can make a meal before her kids head to their sports practices. It can be easier to stay on task when you have a lot to do and don't have time to waste, but if you aren't pressed to get things done, maybe reading the Bible and prayer go by the wayside because you aren't intentional with your time.

Job's example reminds us to look ahead and plan for temptations before they occur, much as coaches prepare their teams for certain situations or generals draw up battle plans. Dwight Eisenhower said, "In preparing for battle I've always found plans are useless, but planning is indispensable."

We are much more likely to make the right choice if we've prepared for the situation. We can't predict how it will occur, but we can predict when conditions may be favorable for falling into sin. For instance, I've found I'm much more likely to lose my temper with my children when I'm in a rush, especially when I'm trying to get somewhere (like to church to teach a class). If I let them know in the evening that I have class in the morning, they might not remember initially, but when I'm scurrying around five minutes before I have to leave and remind them, they'll be on board.

When my husband calls from work when I'm trying to help our youngest with homework, I'm typically abrupt and distracted. Knowing this, it's best to take a minute to answer the phone and let my husband know what's going on and ask if we can talk later.

Look at your schedule for the next weeks and months. What issues are going to come up that may bring added stress, times of loneliness, or significant changes?

What temptations will you be prone to fall into during those times?

The opposite of falling into temptation and embracing evil is to live with integrity. Daniel chapter 6 offers us a great example of a person committed to living with integrity. We're told, **"Now Daniel so distinguished himself among the administrators and the satraps by his exceptional qualities that the king planned to set him over the whole kingdom. At this, the administrators and the satraps tried to find grounds for charges against Daniel in his conduct of government affairs, but they were unable to do so. They could find no corruption in him, because he was trustworthy and neither corrupt nor negligent"** (verses 3,4).

Live with integrity.

Daniel was trustworthy. He did everything he was supposed to do. He wasn't corrupt or negligent. He didn't cut corners. He wasn't making deals under the table. He did what he was supposed to do and didn't do what shouldn't be done. In other words, he was an ideal employee. He was the kind of person you could trust, and he had the king's best interest in mind.

Are we trustworthy to do the things we are asked to do? Maybe we are when we're getting paid, but what about that "honey do" list or the things your elderly parent or neighbor needs? Are you neglecting the not-so-fun parts of your job? Do you skate by doing the very least you can do at home or at work? Do you often look at things and think, "I should really . . ." but then never do?

Be assured there is grace to cover our failings. But it's never too late to start living with integrity and to repent or turn. Not only will your performance at work improve, but as you follow through, it might do wonders for your relationships.

What things have you been putting off because they are difficult or not so fun?

Think of one thing you are doing at work or home that you probably shouldn't be doing. Or think of something that would be a blessing to your family or employer if you didn't do it anymore. Write that down.

Main takeaway: God is good, and we get to bask in his goodness every day. We honor him when we avoid evil and live with integrity. As Christians, or Christ bearers, we uphold his good name when we live in a way that honors him, even if it means loss to us.

About the Writers

Pastor Mike Novotny has served God's people in full-time ministry since 2007 in Madison and, most recently, at The CORE in Appleton, Wisconsin. He also serves as the lead speaker for *Time of Grace*, where he shares the good news about Jesus through television, print, and online platforms. Mike loves seeing people grasp the depth of God's amazing grace and unstoppable mercy. His wife continues to love him (despite plenty of reasons not to), and his two daughters open his eyes to the love of God for every Christian. When not talking about Jesus or dating his wife/girls, Mike loves playing soccer, running, and reading.

Amber Albee Swenson has authored several books and is a regular blogger and podcaster for Time of Grace. Mostly she's amazed at God's goodness, awed by his wisdom and desire to grow her, and continually stretched by his calling in her life. For more details about her ministry, go to amberalbeeswenson.com.

About Time of Grace

Time of Grace is an independent, donor-funded ministry that connects people to God's grace—his love, glory, and power—so they realize the temporary things of life don't satisfy. What brings satisfaction is knowing that because Jesus lived, died, and rose for all of us, we have access to the eternal God—right now and forever.

To discover more, please visit timeofgrace.org or call 800.661.3311.

Help share God's message of grace!

Every gift you give helps Time of Grace reach people around the world with the good news of Jesus. Your generosity and prayer support take the gospel of grace to others through our ministry outreach and help them experience a satisfied life as they see God all around them.

Give today at timeofgrace.org/give or by calling 800.661.3311.

Thank you!